Cryptocurrency for Beginners

Building Your Wealth in the Digital Age

Table of Contents

Chapter 1. Introduction

With the dawn of the digital age, a new form of wealth has quietly reshaped the global financial landscape - Cryptocurrency. Our Special Report 'Cryptocurrency for Beginners: Building Your Wealth in the Digital Age' is the guiding light you need to navigate this exciting yet complex space. But don't worry! Even if the term 'Cryptocurrency' sounds daunting, we have made sure that the report walks you through this journey in the simplest and most understandable possible way. Destined not just for math wizards or tech gurus, our report demystifies this digital gold, right from what it is, how it works, to ways you could amass your cryptocurrency fortune. It's like learning a new language, but here, the words are replaced with numbers, and the phrases - with secure digital transactions. Step into the future of wealth and investment with us, and untangle the intricate world of cryptocurrency. Who knows? This report might just be the key to unlock your digital wealth!

Chapter 2. Understanding Cryptocurrency: A Primer

Every successful journey begins with a first step, and the world of cryptocurrency is no different. To fully understand this revolutionary digital asset, one must delve deep into its origins, the underlying technology that powers it, and the various facets of its operation and application. Let us embark on this detailed exploration to truly comprehend the essence and potential of cryptocurrency.

2.1. The Genesis of Cryptocurrency

Cryptocurrency, in its most basic sense, is a kind of digital or virtual currency that utilizes cryptography for security. The journey began in 2008 with the publication of a whitepaper by an individual or a group of individuals under the pseudonym Satoshi Nakamoto. The paper, titled "Bitcoin: A Peer-to-Peer Electronic Cash System," marked the birth of the first cryptocurrency - Bitcoin. It was brought to life as a response to financial turmoil. Its core tenet was to operate in a decentralized fashion, outside the realm of government control and traditional financial institutions, governed instead by a network of peers.

2.2. Understanding Blockchain: Heart of Cryptocurrency

The heart of any cryptocurrency is the technology that supports it - Blockchain. It is a digital ledger or a record-keeping system where a network of computers holds copies of a database. Each computer, or 'node,' stores a copy of the entire blockchain, and all changes to that database i.e., transactions, are updated across every node, conferring transparency and security. Being decentralized, this eliminates the need for a central authority or middlemen to validate transactions.

The blockchain is made up of 'blocks', and each block contains a certain number of transactions. Once a block reaches a predetermined size, it is added to the blockchain. It's essential to note that all blocks are linked - each new block contains a reference to the previous block through a unique code called a hash, which makes the blockchain incredibly secure and practically tamper-proof.

2.3. Mining Magic: How New Cryptocurrencies are Born

One of the distinctive elements of most cryptocurrencies is their creation, a process known as mining. Miners dedicate their computing resource to solve complex mathematical algorithms, in effect validating new transactions and adding them to the blockchain. As a reward, they receive new units of that cryptocurrency, thus ensuring the circulation of new coins. This is an essential aspect of cryptocurrencies like Bitcoin, which have a cap on the total number that will ever exist.

After the blockchain verifies the transactions, they become indisputable - unmodifiable. Therefore, the aspect of finality characterizes cryptocurrency transactions as they can't be reversed once confirmed.

2.4. The Role of Cryptocurrency Wallets

Think of a cryptocurrency wallet as a digital wallet to store your virtual wealth. These wallets do not store the actual cryptocurrencies but the digital codes or keys (public and private keys) related to them. A Public key is similar to your bank account number, which you share with others to receive funds, while a private key is like your ATM pin, which you keep secret to authorize transactions. Losing your private keys could mean losing your cryptocurrency, reinforcing the importance of secure storage.

2.5. The World of AltCoins

While Bitcoin was the first cryptocurrency, it is far from the only one. As of now, more than 5,000 different cryptocurrencies are traded publicly, collectively called 'Altcoins' or alternative coins. These include prominent names like Ethereum, Ripple's XRP, Litecoin, and many others, each with its unique features, use cases, and underlying technologies.

2.6. Cryptocurrency as an Investment

The potential for high returns has attracted investors to the field of cryptocurrency. But it's crucial to remember that the crypto market is subject to extreme volatility. As with any investment, due diligence is of utmost importance. It's also essential to diversify investments and not invest more than you can afford to lose.

2.7. Legal and Regulatory Environment

The legal treatment of cryptocurrencies varies greatly around the world. Some nations have embraced them, while others have banned them outright. Investing in cryptocurrency involves considering the regulatory environment, which can affect the value and legality of particular cryptocurrencies.

Even as the world is slowly unraveling the mysteries of cryptocurrency, it is reshaping our understanding of money and value. However, successful navigation through this digital terrain requires an apt understanding of its intricacies. As daunting as it might seem, decrypting the cryptocurrency realm could lead to unlocking your digital wealth. The world is evolving, and so are our currencies. Welcome to the future of wealth and investment!

Chapter 3. The Birth of Bitcoin: A History

In the late part of 2008, amidst a global financial crisis, an unfamiliar name surfaced on an obscure mailing list frequented by a few cryptographers. The name was "Satoshi Nakamoto," and the message he sent heralded the birth of a new form of digital currency - Bitcoin.

3.1. The Genesis Reveal

Satoshi Nakamoto announced on the Cypherpunk mailing list the release of a new paper titled "Bitcoin: A Peer-to-Peer Electronic Cash System." This paper introduced the concept of a decentralized currency free from government intervention or control. Arguably, it came as a result or perhaps a reaction to the 2008 financial crisis when trust in banks and financial institutions had plummeted to an all-time low.

The seminal document laid out the premise of Bitcoin. It discussed how digital signatures offer a solution to the problem of online payments, but the absence of a mediator or central authority posed significant challenges, like the issue of double-spending.

3.2. Peek into the Paper

The solution proposed in the paper was innovative - a publicly viewable ledger called the blockchain. Every transaction would be chained to this ledger in the form of blocks, and that blockchain would maintain a history of every transaction ever made. This transparent public record neutralized the risk of double-spending as every transaction involving a specific bitcoin could be traced back to its origin. This groundbreaking approach eliminated the need for a trusted third party.

3.3. The First Bitcoin Transaction

On January 3, 2009, the first block - termed the Genesis Block or Block 0 - was mined by Satoshi himself. This block included a reference to a headline from The Times: "Chancellor on brink of second bailout for banks." This has been interpreted as a critique of the instability of the traditional banking system.

The first transaction of Bitcoin occurred on January 12, 2009, when Satoshi sent 10 bitcoins to Hal Finney, a developer and one of the earliest supporters of Bitcoin. This transaction wasn't just the first for Bitcoin, but for the entire cryptocurrency industry.

3.4. Who is Satoshi Nakamoto?

The identity of Satoshi Nakamoto remains one of the biggest mysteries in the world of technology. Despite numerous attempts to unmask him (or her, or them), the creator's true identity has never been conclusively confirmed. This anonymous character disappeared from the online community in 2010. Before leaving, Satoshi handed Gavin Andresen the control of the source code repository and network alert key, effectively making him the lead developer of Bitcoin. The last message from his validated email account was sent on April 23, 2011, stating: "I've moved on to other things. It's in good hands with Gavin and everyone."

3.5. Mining Explained

Bitcoin was the first cryptocurrency to introduce the concept of 'mining.' Individuals called 'miners' solve intricate mathematical problems that validate transactions. For this service, they are rewarded with bitcoins. This dual-purpose process creates new coins and maintains transaction accuracy within the Bitcoin network. As time progresses, mining Bitcoin has become a complex and resource-heavy task, leading to the formation of mining pools where resources are collectively harnessed.

Miners help maintain the integrity of the Bitcoin network, and the introduction of mining provided a way for early adopters to earn bitcoins without having to purchase them.

3.6. The Emergence of Exchanges

Initially, there was no marketplace to buy and sell bitcoins. The first transaction that involved buying bitcoins with traditional money happened on the Bitcoin forum, where a user agreed to buy 10,000 bitcoins for $50. However, the first recognized exchange platform, BitcoinMarket.com, began to operate in March 2010, allowing individuals to trade Bitcoin for traditional currency.

The next significant development was the infamous Mt. Gox scandal. Mt. Gox was a Japan-based Bitcoin exchange that managed approximately 70% of all Bitcoin transactions worldwide. In 2014, it suffered a massive hack with 740,000 Bitcoin lost or stolen. The scandal sent tremors through the Bitcoin community and nearly spelled the doom of Bitcoin.

3.7. Bitcoin's Decade-Long Journey

Since those early days, Bitcoin has traversed a tumultuous journey. Despite several instances of volatility, security issues, and regulatory challenges, its resilience is seen in the fact that it's continued to grow in relevance and usage. Notably, after around a decade of its inception, Bitcoin received institutional recognition, with major players in the finance world opening up to Bitcoin and even offering futures contracts on it.

However, Bitcoin's influential role extends beyond its objective nature as a currency. It has fostered an entire industry of over 2,000 alternative cryptocurrencies, known as 'altcoins,' and mainstream world has started discussing topics like blockchain technology, decentralization, and financial privacy.

The birth and journey of Bitcoin represent a pivotal point in financial history, marking the inception of a completely new form of wealth. This novel approach towards currency and online transactions has potentially remodelled the financial landscape as we know it, launched an entirely new industry, and prompted serious discussions around the role of traditional financial and regulatory institutions in a digital landscape.

This is just the beginning of Bitcoin's story, and much of its future still remains to be written. Whether you're an investor, academic, or curious observer, the rest of this report will delve deeper into its workings and influence on the future of finance and beyond.

Chapter 4. How Cryptocurrencies Work: The Basics of Blockchain

The world of cryptocurrencies is fascinating, complex, and can often be perplexing especially to newcomers. It's like unboxing a new gadget and figuring out each component simultaneously. Understanding the functioning of cryptocurrencies necessitates a basic understanding of the blockchain, an underlying technology that facilitates these digital transactions.

4.1. Understanding the blockchain

Blockchain is the bedrock upon which the grand edifice of cryptocurrencies is built. It is a digital ledger, a distributed database, used to record transactions across numerous computers. It helps in upholding transparency and eliminates the need for any central authority.

The name 'blockchain' itself denotes its function. A 'block' represents digital information stored in a public 'chain'. Each block contains digital information from three categories -

1. The transaction information, including the details of the sender, recipient, and the number of coins.

2. The transaction timestamp.

3. A unique cryptographic code, the hash, linked to the previous block.

4.2. Hash and the linking of Blocks

The term "hash" refers to a unique identifier for each block. Acting as a digital fingerprint, it differentiates one block from another. Even a minor change in a block's information can alter the hash, necessitating the recalculations for subsequent hash sequences.

After completion of a transaction, the information is stored in a block, along with its hash and the previous block's hash. In this way, blocks are linked consecutively, crafting a chain — the blockchain.

4.3. Blockchain and Decentralization

One of the key elements setting blockchain apart is its decentralized nature. Instead of storing all information in a single location (centralized), blockchain records are distributed across a wide network of computers, known as nodes. Each node in the network carries a copy of the complete blockchain. This decentralization ensures that if one node in the network fails or is compromised, the system isn't affected; the remaining nodes continue recording and storing information.

4.4. Mining and the Creation of New Blocks

The process of adding new blocks to the blockchain is known as mining. Cryptocurrency miners use a combination of complex mathematics and computer power to solve complicated computational problems. Once a solution is found, a new block can be added to the blockchain. If several miners solve the puzzle, the first one to solve it gets the privilege.

To incentivize the mining process, miners are rewarded with cryptocurrencies. For instance, Bitcoin miners receive bitcoins as a reward.

4.5. Security in Blockchains

Security in a blockchain rests within its structure. As mentioned before, each block in a blockchain carries the hash of the previous block. This intuitive arrangement makes it difficult for anyone to alter any detail within a block. If someone tries to alter the data, the hash of the block changes. This change further affects every succeeding block and disrupts the entire blockchain.

To successfully manipulate a blockchain, one would need to change the information in the tampered block and all blocks that follow, re-mine them and control more than 50% of the network, known as the 51% attack. The sheer computing power required to do this makes it practically impossible and thus, ensures the blockchain's security.

4.6. Blockchain: More than just Cryptocurrency

While cryptocurrencies are the most known applications of blockchain technology, the technology's potential extends beyond just cryptocurrencies. Its ability to maintain records securely and transparently makes it ideal for record-keeping activities. For example, it can be used in supply chain tracking, voting systems, and even in the real estate market for transparent property deals.

In conclusion, blockchain stands as a revolutionary technology, creating a trustless and decentralized network that underpins different cryptocurrencies. This understanding of how cryptocurrencies function would provide a solid foundation before diving deeper into some specific cryptocurrencies. Remember, cryptocurrencies bring forth a new era of finance that is still in the early stage of development. Hence, continue learning, continue exploring.

Remember, the world of cryptocurrencies is much like an empowered alien technology: it will seem complicated only until you learn the ropes. Once you've grasped the fundamentals, you'll see not only its complexity but also its brilliance. Let this excursion into the mechanics of cryptocurrencies be your first step towards unlocking your digital fortune.

Chapter 5. Cryptocurrency versus Traditional Money: A Comparative Analysis

In order to comprehend the complete paradigm alteration that cryptocurrency brings to the concept of money, we must first understand the conventional financial framework that serves as its primary contrast. This chapter uncovers a comparative analysis between cryptocurrency and traditional money.

Traditional money - often referred to as fiat currency, has been our anchor to economic exchange for centuries. On the contrary, cryptocurrency, as we know it, is a newcomer, having only been introduced in 2009 with Bitcoin's inception. Despite its youth, cryptocurrency has created substantial waves in the global financial ecosystem.

5.1. What is Fiat Currency and How Does it Work?

We hold in our wallets, transactions, and banks the conception of traditional, physical money. Be it the Dollar, Euro, or any other, it is characterized as the medium of exchange recognized and validated by the government of a particular region, country, or economic union. Fiat currency gets its value from the trust and consensus of the people using it – i.e., if we all agree to use and accept Dollars as a form of payment for goods and services, then Dollars will be worth something.

Moreover, this system is centralized, with an authorized body like a central bank regulating the money supply. Importantly, the forces of demand and supply in economics influence this type of currency value. Inflation, interest rates, and economic growth rates are all factors that can shift the value of a fiat currency.

5.2. What is Cryptocurrency and How Does it Work?

Cryptocurrency, at its simplest, is a digital or virtual form of currency that utilizes cryptography for security. It's a decentralized medium of exchange, meaning it operates outside the control of governments and central banks. Bitcoin, launched in 2009, was the inaugural cryptocurrency, but thousands more have followed since. The total value of all cryptocurrencies as of the time of this writing is around $1.6 trillion.

One distinguishing factor of cryptocurrencies is their underlying technology - the blockchain. Its mathematical and cryptographic workings are fascinating, but all you need to remember is that the blockchain is transparent and immutable, and distributed copies of it reside on nodes throughout the network. This decentralization is a key factor that attracts many users to cryptocurrencies.

Furthermore, cryptocurrencies are typically limited in quantity - the total amount of Bitcoin that can ever exist is capped at 21 million, which adds an element of scarcity, similar to precious metals, aiding to maintain value.

5.3. Comparing Storage and Transactions

The basis of storing traditional money is usually in a physical or digital version inside a bank or similar financial institution. Conversely, cryptocurrencies are stored in digital wallets, which can be hardware-based or web-based, with each wallet having a unique address on the blockchain.

When it comes to transacting, while banks and financial institutions mediate and record transactions in conventional money, a collective known as 'miners' do the same for cryptocurrencies. These 'miners' essentially validate and add transactions to the public ledger, i.e., the blockchain, ensuring the security and authenticity of each transaction.

Moreover, while fiat transactions can take a significant amount of time and often incur fees, especially in cross-border transactions, cryptocurrencies can provide a quick, efficient, and low-cost alternative.

5.4. Privacy, Security, and Regulation

A fundamental difference between traditional money and cryptocurrencies lies in the way privacy and security are handled. Fiat currency arrangements involve banks or financial institutions having access to transaction details and individuals' financial histories - an aspect that has been critiqued for privacy reasons. Cryptocurrencies, however, offer a greater degree of pseudonymity. While the transaction details are transparent on the blockchain, the identity of the transacting parties remains obscured with only their wallet addresses being displayed.

As for regulation, traditional money is strictly regulated by central banks and government bodies, whereas the cryptocurrency market is largely unregulated, leading to increased volatility.

5.5. Economic Impact and the Future of Money

The implications of these differences on global economics are profound—the ability to transfer value electronically without the need for a trusted third-party intermediary (like a bank or government) is truly revolutionary.

It is suggested that cryptocurrencies, in their current form, could be a precursor for a future digital form of money that utilizes the same foundational principles of cryptography, blockchain, and decentralization. However, with the inherent volatility, regulatory concerns, and technical sophistication required, it is essential to take an informed approach to engage with cryptocurrencies.

This analysis is not an endorsement or repudiation of cryptocurrencies. Instead, it provides a basic understanding of the contrast between conventional forms of money and this new digital asset, cryptocurrency. One must consider this knowledge when contemplating participation in this innovative financial dimension. The decision ultimately hinges on individual familiarity, risk tolerance, and trust in both cryptocurrency and traditional financial systems.

Chapter 6. Types of Cryptocurrency: Beyond Bitcoin

When it comes to digital wealth and investment, getting familiar with the various types of cryptocurrencies is crucial. You may be familiar with Bitcoin, the granddaddy of all cryptocurrencies, but there is a world beyond that waiting to be explored. So, let's dive deeper to broaden your understanding of the different kinds of cryptocurrencies available in the market today.

6.1. Major Cryptocurrencies

There are approximately 4000 cryptocurrencies out there. Nonetheless, here are some major ones that you must become well-versed with.

Bitcoin (BTC)

It would be impossible to discuss digital currencies without speaking about Bitcoin. Launched in 2009, Bitcoin was the first cryptocurrency and continues to be the most valuable and influential.

Ethereum (ETH)

Ethereum is the second most valuable cryptocurrency and was launched in 2015. Unlike Bitcoin, which is merely a digital currency, Ethereum offers more functionality with its smart contract features.

Litecoin (LTC)

Often termed the 'silver to Bitcoin's gold', Litecoin was launched in 2011. It was designed to be a faster version of Bitcoin, with the goal of making digital transactions more efficient.

Ripple (XRP)

Launched in 2012, the main function of Ripple is not cryptocurrency but its digital payment protocol used for both fiat money transfers and cryptocurrency. XRP is its own associated cryptocurrency.

Cardano (ADA)

Launched in 2017 by one of Ethereum's co-founders, Cardano is a blockchain platform that allows smart contracts, similar to Ethereum. The key difference is Cardano's emphasis on regulatory compliance and a layered architecture for extra security.

6.2. Altcoins

Altcoins, a contraction of 'alternative Bitcoins', are all the other cryptocurrencies launched following the success of Bitcoin. Even though Bitcoin remains the leader, altcoins serve as viable alternatives, bringing unique features and utilities to the table.

Monero (XMR)

Monero, launched in 2014, is a privacy-focused cryptocurrency. Unlike Bitcoin and many others, Monero's transactions are untraceable, offering complete privacy to the users.

Chainlink (LINK)

This is a digital token tied to the Chainlink network that connects smart contracts with real-world data, events and payments. The Chainlink token is used to pay for these services within the ecosystem.

6.3. Stablecoins

Stablecoins are a special class of cryptocurrencies that aim to provide price stability by being pegged to some reserve, like fiat currency or gold.

Tether (USDT)

Tether, launched in 2014, is the most prevalent stablecoin. Each USDT is designed to be worth $1, making it stable despite the volatility of the crypto markets.

USD Coin (USDC)

Another dollar-pegged stablecoin, USDC aims to blend the advantages of the crypto world with the relative stability of the US dollar.

DAI

Unlike most stablecoins that are backed by reserves of fiat currency, DAI is backed by cryptocurrency (ETH).

6.4. Tokens

Tokens are a specific type of cryptocurrency that represent an asset or a utility and reside on their own blockchain.

Binance Coin (BNB)

Operating on the Binance Chain, BNB can be used to pay transaction fees on the Binance exchange, participate in token sales and more.

UNI Token - Uniswap

Launched in 2020, UNI is governed by the digital asset protocol Uniswap. Holding UNI tokens lets you participate in governance votes.

Through this voyage, you've touched upon just the tip of the cryptocurrency iceberg. Each type of cryptocurrency introduces new possibilities for innovation and investment. But remember, just as the various currencies have diverse functions and applications, they come with unique sets of risks and returns. So, invest wisely.

This detailed exploration into the types of cryptocurrency is pivotal in building your digital wealth. Now that you are familiar with many cryptos beyond Bitcoin, you are well equipped to forge your unique route in the sprawling, exciting world of cryptocurrency.

Chapter 7. Getting Started: Setting Up Your Digital Wallet

Setting up your digital wallet marks your first step towards exploring the vast existence of cryptocurrencies. This process entails choosing your preferred wallet type, selecting a provider, and subsequently taking security measures to safeguard your newfound digital wealth.

7.1. Understanding Cryptocurrency Wallets

Before progressing further, it's pertinent to understand what a cryptocurrency wallet is. Just like a physical wallet holds your fiat currency, a cryptocurrency wallet stores your digital assets. However, instead of storing physical coins or notes, this wallet keeps a pair of digital keys: one public and one private.

The public key is akin to your bank account number, an address you share with others when receiving crypto funds. On the other hand, the private key is similar to your ATM pin, which you use to authorize transactions. Your private key is confidential and needs to be safeguarded vigilantly to prevent unauthorized access or theft.

7.2. Types of Cryptocurrency Wallets

Various types of cryptocurrency wallets cater to different needs. When choosing one, consider factors such as ease of use, security, convenience, and cost.

1. **Software Wallets** Software wallets are applications to be downloaded onto a device. They come in three subtypes: desktop, mobile, and online. Desktop wallets offer the highest level of security but limit access to the device they're downloaded on. Mobile wallets offer portability, letting you make transactions through your phone. Online wallets are cloud-based, accessible from any device with an internet connection, but they're vulnerable to online hacking.

2. **Hardware Wallets** These physical devices store the user's private keys offline on a specially made hardware device, providing an extra layer of security. They can store multiple cryptocurrencies and protect your assets even if your machine is compromised.

3. **Paper Wallets** As the name suggests, these are physical printouts of your public and private keys. They are immune to cyber-attacks but can be physically lost or damaged.

7.3. Choosing Your Wallet Provider

After identifying your suitable wallet type, you need a reputable provider to offer the service. Wallet providers are aplenty, and it's crucial to pick reliable ones. Look for providers with a strong reputation, high user reviews, robust security features, easy usability, and excellent customer support. Some notable ones include Ledger and Trezor for hardware wallets, Electrum and Exodus for software wallets, and MyEtherWallet for an online wallet.

7.4. Setting Up Your Wallet

Before this process, ensure you have secure internet access, as unprotected networks increase the risk of theft. The specific steps vary between providers but follow these general stages:

1. **Download/ Purchase the Wallet** For software wallets, download

the application from the provider's official website, an app store, or Google Play. Avoid unverified sources that might host malicious software. Hardware wallets need to be purchased from authorized sellers, and paper wallets are usually generated online and printed.

2. **Install the Wallet** Follow the installation guide. In most cases, the app will guide you through each step.

3. **Create Your Wallet** Some wallets ask you to create a new one or import an existing one. Choose to create a new wallet.

4. **Backup Your Wallet** Before proceeding, you'll be requested to backup your wallet. This often involves noting down a recovery phrase (24-word random sequence) which will help you recover your wallet if you forget your password or lose your device.

5. **Set a Strong Password** Use a good mix of uppercase and lowercase letters and include symbols and numbers. Remember, anyone with your password can steal your currency instantly.

6. **Receive Your Public and Private Keys** Your wallet is set up and ready for use. You'll see your public address, which you can give to others when they send you digital currency. Your private key will also be displayed—write it down and store it somewhere safe.

7.5. Securing Your Wallet

Getting your wallet ready is just the half-way point. Safeguarding it is another crucial task since cryptocurrencies attract hackers due to their increasing value and semi-anonymity. Here are some essential security measures:

1. **Private Key Security** Never reveal your private key or the recovery phrase. Losing these can result in loss of control over your assets.

2. **Two-Factor Authentication** Enable 2FA, where you verify your

identity using two different credentials. This can be an SMS, an email, or an app authentication.

3. **Regular Updates** Keep your wallet software up-to-date to ensure you have the latest security enhancements.

4. **Use Reputable Security Tools** Install reliable anti-virus and anti-malware software on devices where you access your wallet.

5. **Separate Wallets** Consider using different wallets for storing and trading. A hardware wallet is ideal for storage, while a mobile or desktop one is suitable for daily transactions.

By securing your digital wallet, you not only preserve your cryptocurrency safely but also establish a strong base for effective crypto trading and investing. Acquainting yourself with different wallet types, providers, security measures, and more might seem taxing at first, but it doesn't take long to grasp. In the end, it's a small price for entering the revolutionary world of cryptocurrencies.

Chapter 8. Buying and Selling Cryptocurrency: A Step-by-Step Guide

Before we delve into the details concerning buying and selling of cryptocurrency, it is essential to underscore that this guide is targeted at ordinary investors and not day traders. As such, we will not delve into matters concerning charts, shorting or stop-loss orders. This guide primarily focuses on guiding an average person on how to start their cryptocurrency journey, including buying, storing and selling.

8.1. Understanding Which Cryptocurrency to Invest In

Not all cryptocurrencies are created equal. There are over 6,000 digital currencies out there, which range from the popular ones such as Bitcoin and Ethereum, to the less known ones. When choosing a cryptocurrency, consider factors such as development team, market capitalization, potential for adoption, and the technology behind the coin.

Remember, creating a balanced portfolio of cryptocurrencies is crucial. Investing everything in one coin is somewhat risky and not advisable.

8.2. Creating a Digital Wallet

Prior to buying any cryptocurrency, you need a place to store it - a digital wallet. Some popular options include online wallets, desktop wallets, mobile wallets, and hardware wallets. Each has their pros and cons. For instance, hardware wallets are known to offer the best security, but they are not free. On the other hand, online wallets are handy for accessing your crypto from anywhere, but they may have security issues. Choose a wallet type that suits your needs and circumstances.

8.3. Selecting a Cryptocurrency Exchange

After setting up your digital wallet, the next step is picking an exchange on which to buy your cryptocurrencies. An exchange is a platform that allows you to trade cryptocurrencies for other assets. Some of the most popular exchanges include Binance, Coinbase and Kraken. Compare their fee structures, security measures and the cryptocurrencies they offer before making your selection.

8.4. Buying Cryptocurrency

The process of buying crypto varies between exchanges, but it's generally straightforward. Most purchasers opt to use their bank account or credit card to buy crypto. Once your payment method is set up, navigate to the 'Buy' section, select the cryptocurrency you want to purchase, enter the amount you want to spend, and click 'Buy'. Remember to always double-check the transaction before confirming.

8.5. Transferring from Exchange to Wallet

After buying your crypto, transfer it from the exchange to your wallet. Keeping your cryptocurrencies in the exchange poses a risk, as exchanges can be prime targets for hackers. To transfer your crypto to your wallet, copy your wallet's address, paste it into the exchange's withdrawal section, enter the amount you want to transfer, and finally confirm the transaction.

8.6. Selling Cryptocurrency

When the time comes to sell your cryptocurrency, this process is just as straightforward as buying. Navigate to the 'Sell' section of the exchange, select the cryptocurrency you want to sell and enter the amount. Next, select the method you want to receive your payment, and finally click 'Sell'.

8.7. Understanding Taxes and Legal Obligations

Remember, you will need to pay tax on any profit you make from selling cryptocurrency. It's crucial to keep a record of all your transactions, including exchanges, sales, and even losses. Many countries treat cryptocurrency as a taxable asset, so ensure you understand the laws in your jurisdiction and comply accordingly.

In summary, buying and selling cryptocurrencies can lead to considerable wealth creation. It's important to understand the process, choose your investments wisely, and keep abreast of the evolving laws governing cryptocurrency. Remember to make judicious decisions, and remember: every investment carries a level of risk, so only invest what you're prepared to lose.

Chapter 9. Risks and Rewards of Cryptocurrency Investing

As with any investment opportunity, cryptocurrency investing carries its own blend of risks and rewards. Understanding these will allow you to make informed decisions, weighing the potential for significant returns against the uncertainty and volatility endemic to the crypto landscape.

9.1. The Allure of High Returns

Cryptocurrency has become synonymous with stories of overnight millionaires. Pair this allure with accessible technology, and you have a perfect storm of investment opportunity. Early investors in Bitcoin, Ethereum, and other digital currencies have seen astronomical returns on their investments that would have taken traditional stocks decades to achieve. As cryptocurrencies mature and increase in acceptance, it's realistic to expect the potential for considerable returns.

Increased accessibility is a crucial driver of the potential for high returns. All you need is a smartphone or computer, and you can buy cryptocurrencies from anywhere in the world. Unlike traditional stocks and shares, there's no need for brokers, which widens the pool of potential investors and, in theory, making the prospects of profits more promising.

9.2. Volatility and Potential for High Rewards

The very nature of cryptocurrencies presents an avenue for high returns. Values can skyrocket in a short period due to the highly volatile nature of the market. The same fluctuations that can wreak havoc on your investment can also create perfect conditions for immense growth. With the right knowledge and trading strategy, you can leverage this volatility.

However, cryptocurrency values are speculative and often unpredictable. Although the potential for high rewards exists and is a significant catalyst for many investors, it's essential to keep in mind that just as crypto can appreciate massively, it can also experience substantial depreciation.

9.3. The Risks: Volatility and Market Uncertainty

While high volatility and market uncertainty offer the potential for high rewards, they also present significant risks. Cryptocurrency prices can fluctick wildly in hours or even minutes. Bitcoin, for instance, has seen its value drop by thousands of dollars in the space of a day. Other digital currencies have followed suit.

These value swings can be driven by factors including technological changes, market manipulation and regulatory news or events. A mere rumor can cause a coin's value to plummet or soar, leading to a profoundly unstable market. Market uncertainty also arises from speculation and the relatively early stage of technology and market development.

9.4. Regulatory Risks

Cryptocurrency operates in a legal grey area, and different countries have dealt with it in different ways. Some have embraced it, some have restricted it, while others are still grappling with what to do. As such, the lack of clear regulatory guidelines poses a significant risk to cryptocurrencies.

Regulatory decisions can reduce or even eliminate the value of a coin. Therefore, as a prospective cryptocurrency investor, it is necessary to keep abreast of ongoing and upcoming changes in your country's cryptocurrency regulation.

9.5. Security Risks

The digital nature of cryptocurrency brings about unique security risks. Hacks and cyber theft have become common in the industry. Moreover, due to the anonymized nature of transactions and limited recovery options, it may be difficult, if not impossible, to recover stolen cryptocurrencies.

Nevertheless, advancements in technology - like the use of hardware wallets and two-factor authentication - can help assuage some of these issues.

9.6. The Risk of Obsolescence

With technology continually evolving, cryptocurrencies face the risk of becoming obsolete. New coins are often introduced with enhanced technology and better features, pushing out old ones. As technology rapidly advances and new developments emerge, keeping pace can be daunting. Investments in older or less technologically advanced cryptocurrencies may risk becoming worthless, presenting yet another risk to consider.

9.7. In Conclusion: Balancing Risk and Reward

Ultimately, investing in cryptocurrency requires balancing potential high rewards with significant risks. Doing your research, understanding market conditions, keeping abreast of regulatory developments, and implementing robust security measures can help navigate the pitfalls of cryptocurrency investing while still seizing its considerable benefits.

The high-risk, high-reward nature of cryptocurrencies makes them particularly suited for those who can afford to lose their investment. Thus, it might be helpful to adopt the old adage in investing: Never invest more than what you can afford to lose. However, with due diligence, understanding and some amount of calculated risk, investing in cryptocurrency could potentially be a very rewarding venture.

Chapter 10. Exploring Cryptocurrency Mining: The Alternate Route to Digital Wealth

In the universe of cryptocurrency, mining plays a significant role in creating new digital coins and verifying transactions on the blockchain. Yes, mining in the crypto world is a bit different from real-world mining. It doesn't involve sweaty miners with heavy tools, but powerful computers solving complex equations.

Understanding Cryptocurrency Mining: Fundamentals === Let's start at the very beginning. Cryptocurrency mining is the process in which transactions for different forms of cryptocurrency are verified and added to the blockchain, a decentralized ledger. It is also the method by which new crypto coins are created. The whole process involves compiling recent transactions into blocks, solving a complex mathematical problem and adding the solved block to the blockchain.

In a more technical sense, miners use software to solve cryptographic puzzles. If the puzzle is solved, the miner can add a block to the blockchain and get rewarded with some cryptocurrency.

The Tools of the Trade === To start mining, you need a few essential tools:

1. Computer hardware.

2. Mining software.

3. A bitcoin wallet.

4. Stable internet connection.

Mining requires significant computational power. When Bitcoin first started, it was possible to mine with a standard home PC. But as more people joined the network, the difficulty of the puzzles increased. Now you would need a high-powered computer specially built for mining, known as a 'mining rig', to find it lucrative.

The mining software is your digital pickaxe, assisting you in solving the required algorithms. It connects your hardware to the blockchain and the mining pool. Your cryptocurrency wallet is the digital equivalent of your real-world wallet, a secure digital space to store your mined coins.

Types of Cryptocurrency Mining === There are a few different ways to mine cryptocurrencies:

1. Solo Mining: This is the basic form of mining where a miner sets up his hardware and software to mine alone. While the rewards (getting the whole block reward plus fees of transactions compiled) can be more substantial, the chances of solving a block are very thin due to the enormous number of miners.

2. Pool Mining: Miners join their resources to form 'pools' to solve blocks more efficiently. The reward is then split among the pool members according to who has contributed what amount of work.

3. Cloud Mining: This involves renting mining power from a service provider, who has dedicated facilities with powerful machines. Here, you don't need to invest in a mining rig; instead, you pay a fee for using someone else's rig.

Proof of Work vs. Proof of Stake === Two important consensus mechanisms in the context of cryptocurrency mining are 'Proof of Work (PoW)' and 'Proof of Stake (PoS)'.

Proof of Work is the original method used by cryptocurrencies such as Bitcoin. It involves miners who use computational energy to solve mathematical problems and add new transactions to the blockchain.

Proof of Stake, on the other hand, is a newer concept. It selects the validator (miner) not based on computational power, but the amount of cryptocurrency a miner holds, and often the age of that holding. PoS is considered a 'greener' alternative as it requires far less energy to maintain.

The Rewards of Mining === Miners are rewarded with cryptocurrency for each block they mine. The reward systems work differently in different cryptocurrencies.

In Bitcoin, for instance, the block reward halves approximately every 4 years in an event known as 'halving'. As of 2020, the block reward stands at 6.25 Bitcoins. However, Ethereum, another major cryptocurrency, uses a different approach, implementing an "Ethash" algorithm to reduce the reward gradually.

Final Thoughts === While cryptocurrency mining can be lucrative for some, it isn't always the case for everyone. The high energy requirements, the initial investment for a suitable mining rig, fluctuations in the price of cryptocurrencies, and competition among miners mean that mining isn't always profitable. However, if you can effectively balance these factors, mining might just be your path to earn some digital wealth.

Chapter 11. Future of Cryptocurrency: Trends and Predictions

The world of cryptocurrency is in constant flux, with new technologies and market trends continually redefining its future outlook. Some envision a future where cryptocurrencies reinvent the financial system, while others see cryptocurrencies playing secondary roles, such as cross-border transfers and remittances. Let's delve into the potential future trends and predictions of cryptocurrencies.

11.1. The Advent of Central Bank Digital Currencies

Central Bank Digital Currencies (CBDCs) are a futuristic vision of national currencies, that may become real sooner than many think. Central banks around the world are studying the benefits and risks surrounding digital currencies, given their increased prominence in financial transactions. Research from the Bank of International Settlements reveals that as of early 2021, around 80% of central banks have begun exploring CBDCs, and some have embarked on pilot projects.

The adoption of CBDC can potentially decrease cash handling costs, increase financial inclusion, and reduce cross-border transaction time. However, crucial challenges such as privacy, cybersecurity, and operational risks need to be addressed before making CBDC a reality.

11.2. Cryptocurrency: A Primary Financial Asset

Cryptocurrencies currently occupy a unique place in the financial ecosystem - they are traded widely like securities, used as a form of payment, and sometimes treated as a commodity. In the future, they might find increasing prominence as primary financial assets or a value store, similar to other commodities such as gold.

Such a development would require more stability in cryptocurrency valuations, and potentially, increased regulatory supervision. This shift would also necessitate changes in the broader financial industry, particularly among banks, stock exchanges, and financial service providers.

11.3. Regulatory Evolution

We see a trend towards strengthened and well-defined regulatory policies. This may provide legal certainty to stakeholders without stifling innovation. As regulatory jurisdictions across the globe come to terms with the unique features of cryptocurrencies, it's likely we'll witness a greater level of international cooperation, mainly around Anti-Money Laundering (AML) and Know Your Customer (KYC) norms.

However, the challenge lies in forming regulative norms, for one, that don't inhibit the development of the cryptocurrency industry while simultaneously balancing the need for protection against financial crimes, fraud, and cyber threats.

11.4. Adoption in Micro and Macro Transactions

Cryptocurrencies are expected to influence both ends of the transaction size spectrum. On the micro side, the aim is to make transactions as small as fractions of a cent possible, which is often termed as 'nano' or 'micro' payments. Cheaper transaction costs and the ability to handle mass simultaneous transactions set the stage for the adoption of cryptos in everyday micro-transactions.

On the other side, cryptocurrencies can be used for macro transactions, such as large investment transfers or cross-border transactions. Mass adoption of cryptocurrencies in this area could lead to more efficient and cost-effective transactions when dealing with large sums or international boundaries.

11.5. Adoption of Decentralized Finance

Decentralized Finance or DeFi represents a major future trend in the crypto space. A vast domain, DeFi leverages blockchain technologies and cryptographic assets to displace traditional financial intermediaries. DeFi platforms offer several financial services such as lending and borrowing, asset trading, yield farming, insurance, and more, all managed by smart contracts on a blockchain network.

This field is still quite nascent, but considering the pace at which it's growing, DeFi can potentially transform how finance functions. Implementing DeFi on a broad scale can have profound implications on banks, insurance companies, and other financial service providers, possibly leading to a comprehensive democratization of finance.

11.6. Integration of AI and Blockchain Technology

The collision of blockchain and AI opens possibilities for enhanced efficiency, automation, and security in financial transactions. Blockchain technology can help make AI more coherent and understandable, while AI can manage and operate blockchain more efficiently than humans or any earlier conventional system.

We're only just beginning to understand the implications of combining AI and blockchain. Although the synergistic potential is immense, the lack of universal standards poses a significant challenge.

Cryptocurrency's future incorporates a broad spectrum of possibilities. The advent and successful application of CBDCs, the classification of cryptocurrencies as primary financial assets, regulations' evolution, micro and macro transactions, the rise of DeFi, and integration of AI and blockchain are some of the foreseeable trends shaping the future. Understanding these trends will be crucial in making informed decisions on how and when to incorporate cryptocurrencies into your investment portfolio or business operations.

www.ingramcontent.com/pod-product-compliance
Lightning Source LLC
Chambersburg PA
CBHW071612270726
48661CB00019B/3117